17/06

Trompe L'Oeil
Sea and Sky

Ursula E. and Martin Benad

Trompe L'Oeil
Sea and Sky

Translated by Ingrid Li

W. W. Norton & Company
New York • London

Copyright © 2004 by Deutsche Verlags-Anstalt GmbH, München
English translation copyright © 2005 by W. W. Norton & Company, Inc.

Originally published in German as HIMMEL UND MEER: Studienreihe Illusionsmalerei

For information about permission to reproduce selections from this book, write to Permissions, W. W. Norton & Company, Inc., 500 Fifth Avenue, New York, NY 10110

Composition by Ken Gross
Design by a. visus. Michael Hempel, Munich
Manufacturing by Jütte-Messedruck GmbH, Leipzig

Library of Congress Cataloging-in-Publication Data

Benad, Ursula.
    [Himmel und Meer. English]
    Trompe l'oeil sea & sky / Ursula E. and Martin Benad; translated by Ingrid Li.
         p.   cm.
    Includes bibliographical references and index.
    ISBN 0-393-73171-5 (pbk.)
    1. Decoration and ornament--Trompe l'oeil. 2. Skies in art. 3. Sea in art. I. Title: Trompe l'oeil sea and sky. II. Benad, Martin. III. Title.

NK1590.T76 B4513   2005
745.4—dc22   2004057579

ISBN 0-393-73171-5 (pbk.)

W. W. Norton & Company, Inc., 500 Fifth Avenue, New York, N.Y. 10110
www.wwnorton.com
W. W. Norton & Company Ltd., Castle House, 75/76 Wells St., London W1T 3QT

0 9 8 7 6 5 4 3 2 1

Contents

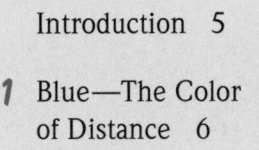

Introduction

The omnipresence of television and magazines has trivialized images. The effect of this flood of pictures is that we have seen it all, yet we don't really know any of it. Painting or drawing becomes an act of resistance. Looking at the world with our own eyes and creating a painted representation of what we see is to form a personal connection with things. Representational painting seems archaic to many, but it is an important developmental stage for the individual and cannot be skipped just because one happens to be born after Kandinsky, Malevich, and Mondrian.

Even representational painting never shows objects as they really are, but always in a particular view, a specific form, and with a unique expression. The artist animates the motifs; similarly, we experience nature as animated if we approach it with an open mind.

Skies and seas are motifs with a "message" that most people interpret in a similar way. The sky is expansive; the ocean leads into the distance. The blue yonder has no borders; you can get lost in it, dissolve in it. There is no end to reach; what lies behind the horizon remains unknown. The ocean fascinates: transparent little waves splash around our feet, but deeper down the water seems unfathomable, mysterious, even dangerous. As the waves roll in, so the soul manifests itself in waking consciousness, never revealing its full depth. The sky is of course a metaphor of spiritual life.

The painter has to deal with the challenge of space and time. Waves are to water as clouds are to sky. Both are ephemeral; their shapes are forever forming and dissolving. Clouds and waves depict time, movement, and life itself. Painted waves are most convincing when the viewer can see how they appeared a little while ago and what they will look like in a moment. Painted clouds are most attractive when their structure is apparent, when it is clear where the wind will blow them next and where they are coming from. With birds in the sky the painter signals awake awareness, with fish in the underwater world a dreamy state of consciousness. Each painting is much more than just representation of objects. It points beyond itself.

About painting from photographs: Purists insist on painting only from nature. But there is no ocean in the mountains, no blue sky on a dreary November day, and watercolors cannot be painted under water. The old masters had sketchbooks; we have photographs, but of course, this does not mean that sketching on location is obsolete. But if we use techniques like overhead projection of photos or trace images on a 1:1 scale, no moral scruples are necessary. There simply is no reason any artist should have to hide the use of such tools. The brilliant Renaissance painter Andrea Pozzo used cutting-edge technology when he stretched a grid of strings and projected the lines into the dome of St. Ignatius. Were he alive today, he would probably use a laptop and a laser level.

We wish you much joy
in all your creative endeavors!

Ursula and Martin Benad
Munich, Spring 2004

1 Blue—The Color of Distance

2 (page 5)
Detail of figure 62, page 46.

3
Detail of figure 9, page 8.

Sky and sea are manifestations of blue. Goethe called the color blue "a charming nothing." But while "nothing" is invisible, blue, the "charming nothing," has a definite effect on the senses. Blue demands that we look, and when we do, we perceive distance, detachment, infinity, and a drifting away . . .

When we view a work of art, we interpret large interconnected areas of blue as sky or water with ease. A light blue rectangle with a dark frame and dark cross bars we read as clear sky seen through a window. The trompe l'oeil painter works with this routine equation of blue and sky. Blue makes walls and ceilings disappear and suggests that a viewer is not within the confines of a building but in wide open space. The illusion is enhanced if blue is applied in glazes and subtle nuances, and if it contrasts with sharper contours in the foreground, where objects appear close and substantial through the use of light–dark contrasts.

Figure 4 shows two walls, 46 and 52 ft (14 and 16 m) high. They enclose a small courtyard that is flanked by two 66 ft (20 m) high buildings. The yard belongs to a restaurant whose owner planned to use it for outdoor seating. One potential customer who visited the space said he felt as if he had been thrown into a well. He thought that no one could ever possibly feel comfortable there. A mural saved the space: it opens the facade in several places and creates views of the sky (figures 5 and 6). A painted glass dome, seen from below in perspective, shows more blue sky. The walls are nowhere to be seen; the oppressive weight has literally dissolved into thin air!

4
Concrete canyon: A small courtyard 36 ft (11 m) square is surrounded by walls.

5
The blue of the painted sky creates space. The gray-blue of painted window panes allows the eye to see beyond the actual wall.

6
Sky blue was applied as a glaze in several layers, contrasting with the architecture's crisp lines.

7, 8
From sleeping nook to airy loft: the mountains contribute to the success of the illusion. Space is experienced through the contrast of near and far.

The bed in figure 7 stands close to the wall in a little room. It doesn't seem oppressive with its walls painted in a friendly shade of ochre, the baseboards in a light green. But figure 8 shows the same room after it has been repainted. Who would want to return to the blank walls after a night in this loft? A soft breeze seems to move outside, and what could induce sleep more peacefully than a few little clouds gliding off into the distance? Here, too, the space almost creates itself. The clear light and dark lines of the window grid contrast with the pale blue sky, which leads the eye into the distance.

The color blue has the power to open up confines, and figures 9 and 10 illustrate one more example. A plasterboard-paneled room in a basement was turned into a relaxing and inviting oasis where the walls are "dissolved" by the sky. The half-columns in the foreground enhance the effect of illusionistic spaciousness. Tangible, nearby objects are the necessary counterpoints to the experience of undefined distance.

9 (above)
Blue breaks down walls effortlessly.

10
A low-ceilinged room in a basement with little potential as a traditional recreation spot.

Taking existing architecture into account

Illusionistic painting, or trompe l'oeil, changes rooms by reinterpreting painted walls. Every wall is the boundary of a room; trompe l'oeil turns walls into doorways to an imaginary world. The viewer should experience this world as part of the real world and should not immediately exclaim, "This is just a painting!" The passage between the real and the imagined can be traversed almost unnoticeably if certain elements connect both worlds. Most important, these are walls, ceilings, and floors. It seems reasonable to continue the floor the viewer stands on into the painting. When the real floor reappears as a painted floor, it functions as a bridge leading into the imaginary world. The design in figure 11 (top, at left) shows actual floor tiles and their painted counterparts acting as continuation. The terrace lies above beach level; it seems as if one has to walk down an incline to get to the beach. The apparent difference in elevation "cuts off" the beach and connects the fictional exterior world to the observer's space in a credible manner. Figure 12 shows the same room without the terrace. Here the painted beach is directly adjacent to the floor of the room. It creates an odd and highly unlikely situation: Who has ever seen a room with a missing wall and a floor that abuts the beach?

A second bridge is created for the viewer by the wall that carries the image. In the first design it remains a wall reduced to two narrow segments on the left and right sides supporting an arch. Painterly means create architectural space for an imaginary reality. This frame is credible, even though it is only painted and connected to the real space, and this allows the viewer to consider the distant vista a reality as well. At least the viewer has the option to consider this view a reality, and that is the most important part. Without such a frame—see figure 2—the ceiling of the room meets the painted sky directly, and the line along which ceiling and wall meet marks a demarcation between real space and painted sky. The left and right walls of the room seem to end in open space in a fairly abstract manner. The painting resembles wallpaper because the room that it

was meant to expand has not been taken into consideration at all.

Illusionistic paintings without built-in bridges to reality quickly turn into naive art, and if the painter also succumbs to some typical beginners' errors—see figure 12—the result may be lovable or charming, but it is hardly trompe l'oeil!

Matching the style of the house

Illusionistic painting often falls victim to a particular danger: the temptation of decoration. Rooms are stuffed with content that has no relation to the room itself or its inhabitants. Why would a peacock strut through a modern bathroom? During the seventeenth and eighteenth centuries peacocks, putti, allegories, and the like were in fashion, but do you have to quote the visual vocabulary of the time just because you use one of its glorious art forms, the mural?

Voluminous balustrades, antique marble columns, Greek temples, and Roman busts are all images from the past that can be quoted if a certain style from the past is to be invoked or newly interpreted. But when these images are imported without reflection into modern hotels and private bathrooms, the result is often kitsch. Motifs are treated like decals—stereotypical reproductions empty of any individual expression. Marble balustrades have their place in paintings, ideally where real balustrades are continued in the painting, or where they might fit in but could not be realized as real architectural elements. One can always dream. . . . In most cases, however, it is best to match the style

13, 14
Black-and-white rendering of the motifs in figures 15 and 16. The perspective is constructed with precision. Both images can be used as basis for further variations.

11 (page 9)
Design for a mural in a room that has to be expanded illusionistically.

12 (page 9)
Naive art instead of illusionistic art. The connection to the actual space is missing. The palm tree grows directly from the baseboard, the lamps are screwed to the sky. The motifs come from schematic patterns rather than from natural models: a lonely sausage-shaped cloud floats above two triangular islands. Exactly in the middle of the painting, balanced on the horizon, a bathtub boat floats proudly. Given its distance from the viewer, the mast would have to be 820 ft (250 m) high. A permanent breaker crowned with white foam crashes down at the feet of the viewer only to drain away in too many too-small bays.

15, 16

Two designs for the same room using the same compositional grid. Only the style and the forms differ. Figure 15 shows a version that would be suited to most modern surroundings; figure 16 seems more attractive at first glance.

of the building and to incorporate elements that match the existing interior, support and enhance it, and show it to its best advantage. Figures 13, 14, 15, and 16 show two designs for the same room situation. One uses the vocabulary of cool concrete and is meant for a contemporary building; the other, a softer, classical variation, transcends changing styles and modern forms.

The designs in figures 17 and 19 illustrate two different approaches to the treatment of a room (figure 18 shows the room before it was painted). Both designs enlarge the indoor swimming pool area by visually opening an end and side wall with a view of a landscape with sky and sea. Both incorporate real architectural elements into the painting but they do it from different viewpoints. The "Greek Bath Temple" variation focuses on the columns in the foreground of the pool and repeats them in the mural. The design principle of horizontal elements and a figure frieze is of classical Greek origin and is part of the structure itself as well as in the painting. Thus real space and painted space blend into a harmonious whole. The modern interpretation of the hall focuses on blocklike divisions of the window facade and develops that further in the painting. Real space and painted space are also connected through the design of the columns, whose black-and-white marble reappears as painted mosaic on the imaginary terrace. A (real) potted plant has a painted counterpart, and the real wall lights are echoed in the row of painted columns. Reality and illusion refer to each other and make it almost impossible for the viewer to draw the line between them.

Suspending time

Unlike movable panel paintings, whose frames signify their independent status, murals are tied into the context of architecture. In a mural the wall can be both frame and support, as examples have shown. Since walls are enduring structures, illusionistic murals should have characteristics of permanence. The wide ocean, the blue sky, the palm tree, all might look tomorrow as they do today, and are therefore credible subject matter for a mural. On the other hand, a surfer in close-up as he struggles to maintain his balance is a less credible choice. The represented moment is brief, but the wall is patient. Tomorrow the surfer will still be wobbling; ten years may pass, and his struggle with equilibrium remains frozen into a presence that will never release him. Such paintings may be realistic, but they are not convincing illusionism.

17

A design suggestion for a bathroom in Greco-Roman style. It uses the round columns and staircase of the architectural space and creates variations of it in the painting, a congruency that justifies the theme in spite of the historic dissonance.

18

The room in figures 17 and 19 without painting.

19

The same room in a modern outfit. The point of departure is the linear cubism that many people today find more accessible than round and playful forms. Thus, such a design scheme is often called "modern."

20, 21

Vase with seashells. An unusual still life that invites contemplation.

What about foaming whitecaps? These too are snapshots of particular moments. Are we advocating a dead, never-changing world in which no flowers ever bloom (they last only a few days), no birds sing, and no clouds sail? The size and importance of the represented object are of the essence here. If a single dramatic breaker is chosen as the main subject, the illusion will fail. If the ocean itself is the subject, it will persuade, even if many foam-capped waves fill the middle ground and surfers frolic in the distance. Even dramatic scenes full of motion can be absorbed into the main image, enliven it, and give it individual character. The impression of the whole remains archetypal, timeless, and general. While history paintings focus on a particular moment in time and aim to preserve certain events, such as a sea battle, for posterity, illusionistic paintings represent what is timeless and continuous.

In this context still lifes are important elements. They show continuity and focus attention. Viewers spend time looking at them and this careful attention creates a presence that endows the timeless image with life. See how much interest can be lavished on the shells in a vase (figures 20 and 21) just to explore their forms and patterns.

Besides still lifes there are also narrative scenes, which create the charm of trompe l'oeil paintings. More often, they offer not a complete narrative but a few hints that invite the viewer to decipher and complete the story. Figure 22 shows some kind of a beach party, but we cannot be sure if it is a child's birthday or a moonlight disco party. The scene's charm comes from the tension

between the "eternal" ocean and the fleeting character of the depicted episode. The beach party painting is not a mural but a large-scale canvas. The painted doorframe is also the picture frame, and the work could be hung in many different houses without losing its trompe l'oeil character.

Hinting at certain situations can easily be overdone and become an intellectual game of its own. It is tempting to add a very realistic bikini top to the trunk of the palm tree in figure 138 (page 82), as if someone had just tied it there. In large and authoritative paintings particularly, such touches can be a quick and easy way to earn a laugh—where might the owner of the garment be?—but it is rarely an enduring asset.

Beach party. The writing in mirror image imagines guests who look in "from the outside." This painting leaves room for the viewer's imagination.

Another way of dealing with the central topic of passing time in illusionist paintings is through simple minimalist representation. The two "chairs at the beach" in figures 145 and 146 (pages 86, 87) could hardly be any more reduced. The unadorned surfaces and lines of the architecture, the light and shadow of the objects make time "stand still." The moment turns into eternity the more severely and photographically correct every detail is rendered. This has to do with the psychology of perception: these images don't primarily show objects like chairs on a terrace, but rather a type of perception. The view of the artist meets the view of the observer, who becomes conscious of his own mode of perception.

Conventional, classic trompe l'oeil as it is found in spas and hotels makes no demands of the viewer. No thinking is required; it is only necessary to enjoy the image and relax and refuel. Meanwhile time stands still or moves backward. No new events demand attention; what has happened already can be appraised; body and soul can regenerate. What could be better suited to such a task than timeless themes beyond the fray of daily life, untouched by the worries of the moment?

Creating Space

The perspective grid

Sometimes the intended effect does not unfold. There are two common reasons. Clouds, waves, islands, mountains, ships, or birds in the distance are painted too large, or clouds and waves that should be almost directly above or below the viewer are shown in a side view. The perspective grid in figure 24 can help to clarify the connections. Imagine the grid as floor or ceiling tiles. The horizontal lines are the same distance from one another in reality. This is also true for the rays that converge at the vanishing point. They too are parallel and equidistant from each other in reality. If you could stand on any of the floor tiles looking straight up or down, the tile above or below would appear as a perfect square without distortion. This special case is never represented in the grid, but the tiles in the foreground appear almost square—namely, as slightly foreshortened trapezoids. Looking toward the horizon, only the side edges of the tiles are visible. Perfect bird's eye or worm's eye views are not possible because the horizon represents eye level, and any object along the horizon therefore lies exactly at eye level. All objects shown lie between the two extremes of "only side view" or "only bird's eye or worm's eye view." The farther away they are, the more we see them from the side; the closer they are, the more likely becomes a bird's eye or worm's eye view.

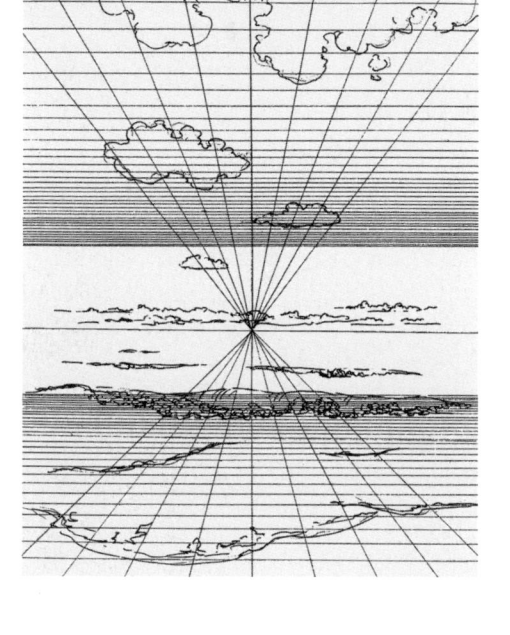

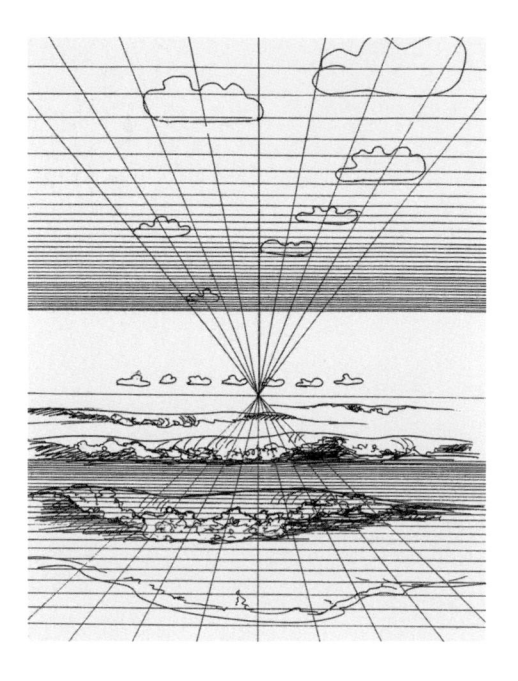

23 (page 17)
See caption 122, page 76.

24
Perspective grid with clouds and waves in appropriate proportions.

25
The same grid with clouds that seem to float above the viewer's head but are seen in side view. The waves are too big for their distance.

A horizontal grid can never be completed all the way to the horizon. The lines move infinitely close to each other. The same principles can be applied to a cloudy sky. Distant clouds appear closer to each other or as a narrow strip, even if the clouds are evenly distributed across the sky. The same is true for waves. If we could clearly identify one wave among all others near the horizon, it would have to be many miles high in reality.

You must also take into consideration the width of clouds and waves. A wave that can fill the entire width of the foreground would occupy only a fraction of that space farther back in the picture. With the grid it is possible to arrange and compare units of length correctly. It helps to clarify relationships and it makes obvious how quickly things in the background are fore-shortened.

Figure 25 illustrates two common mistakes. The clouds are shown in correct proportions, but they are shown in side view while they float directly above the viewer. The wave in the fore-ground seems tiny and harmless compared to the ferocious breaker further back in the ocean—a highly unlikely scenario.

Height

With the grid in figure 24 it is not possible to depict things directly below or above the viewer. To get such a view, the viewer's head, or at least his or her eyes, would have to move and that, by definition, would change the vanishing point away from the previously established horizon. To create a mural with a view into a dome-shaped sky, you would have to show clouds around the zenith, as shown in figures 26 and 27. The pano-rama that can be experienced at a beach depends on an unobstructed field of vision. In figure 26 the field of vision is an angle of 140 degrees. The viewer perceives the sky above and the sand below because the viewer is not restricted to one fixed point of view, but is able to move his or her

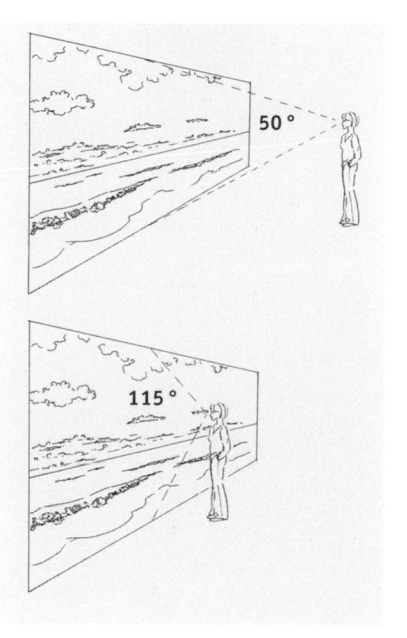

head and eyes to combine the images. A mural might aim to create the same grand impression that this observer enjoys, but there is generally only a 45- to 60-degree field of vision available in which to approximate the effect of the original scene. The closer the observer is to the wall, the more the field of vision is filled by it, which means the viewer has to look up or down to see the entire image. Even if a mural consisting primarily of sky views does not show a 140-degree field of vision, or even one of 100 degrees or less, it should be clear by now that any imposing sky painted on a wall must be shown in "wide angle" (figures 28 and 29) and include portions that would actually be located on the ceiling.

The same is true for ceiling murals by analogy. They must show not just the sky seen directly above the viewer but also sections that would naturally be located on the upper parts of

26
Field of vision of a viewer at the beach . . .

27
. . . and inside a room with a mural.

28
A vertical field of vision of 140 degrees is only possible with a wide-angle lens.

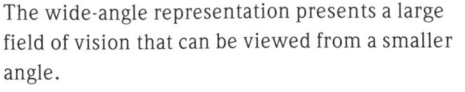

The wide-angle representation presents a large field of vision that can be viewed from a smaller angle.

the walls. The only thing that should never be shown on a ceiling is the natural horizon line. A guideline for the placement of the horizon on the wall is to locate it where it falls in nature: at the eye level of the observer. The eye level of a very tall viewer standing in an 8 ft (2.5 m) high room will clearly be near the upper edge of the walls. Under such a circumstance, how is a balanced composition possible, and where is there any space for the sky? Another danger is that a "rising" ocean will surround the viewer and create the impression of standing in a bathtub. Furthermore, what will happen if the viewer sits down, reclines, or descends into a pool? There are many good reasons to choose the level of the horizon line freely or to adjust it to look best under specific circumstances. Adhering strictly to the rules of linear perspective ignores the fact

Panorama assembled from three images.

that large murals are rarely viewed from a fixed position the way one usually looks at smaller paintings. The viewer looks around, walks around, and the actual horizon line moves accordingly and may or may not match the horizon at which painted sea and sky meet. It is practical to set the horizon slightly lower than geometry would suggest.

The result is a feeling of overview, as if you stood on a tower to look out over the land without actually lowering your gaze. The natural horizon also moves downward in the field of vision if the viewer lifts his or her head to look at the clouds. A number of attractive clouds can invite the raising of heads and thus a simultaneous perception of a lower horizon line. Seascapes afford considerable freedom because there are no converging lines to deal with that might otherwise define a clear vanishing point on a geometric horizon line.

Murals that assume that the viewer's position is slightly above sea level are usually perceived as pleasant. Murals surrounding pools often use slightly raised viewpoints as well, as is evident in the terrace designs of the previous chapter. If a horizon line lies at a height of 31 in (80 cm), it might represent an actual horizon height (eye above sea level) of 65 ft (20 m), which would be evident in the fact that a 49 ft (15 m) high tree or house could be seen from above and would not rise above the horizon line. Spectacular effects can be achieved if the illusionistic painting does not show the natural horizon at all. The viewer is led to imagine floating above the clouds or drifting below the surface of the sea.

Width

The wide-angle effect does not work for the length of a wall because a viewer can simply walk back and forth in front of it, as one walks back and forth at a beach. Only the dimensions of any interior space are considerably smaller. The entire circumference of the room is seen not from a fixed point of view but from an ever-changing one. While the height of the horizon remains constant, the vanishing points move together with the viewer toward the left or the right. Note that the mural will not show three discrete sets of central perspective renditions even if there are three main viewing positions for the image. Instead, one central representation is chosen and the vanishing points move to exaggerated positions toward the left and the right.

"Foldable Ocean." The horizon appears in a zigzag form on a screen.

The impression of realistic space is created by converging lines, multiple layers, cold–warm contrasts, light–dark contrasts, highlights, cast shadows and form shadows, and sharp and soft lines.

the horizon line between the walls in a zigzag line. Here the tension between the brilliantly painted illusion and the obvious trick is so strong that it completely destroys the trompe l'oeil effect, replacing it with a charming piece of decoration.

Depth

One of the most important questions an illusionistic painter has to deal with is how to create depth. After all, this is the dimension the painted ground lacks. The brief suggestions on linear perspective discusssed earlier (see "Height") will usually suffice for the painter of seascapes, since water is not a geometric object and perspective grids are usually unnecessary. Geometry is only one possible way of creating depth. Figure 34 (page 25), and details in figures 32 and 33 show a number of techniques that can be used in conjunction to produce impressive spatial illusions:

1. *Construction of columns and floor tile with the help of a perspective grid.*
2. *Strong light–dark contrasts* to represent the volume of objects, especially in the foreground (for example, shadows cast by the capitals). The objects seem to be touchable; they have a presence in space.

This rule applies to wide images, while tall and narrow ones are designed with vanishing points closer to the median, as you would expect. The result is that even the edges of such an image can be read without too much distortion.

For the photograph in figure 30 (page 21), three images were combined. The field of vision measures approximately 180 degrees. Even a view like that can be achieved in a mural, but architectural details become extremely difficult to include because the view moves first toward the east, then to the west, and all that is shown on just one photograph. A mural rendition of such an image should be represented on two walls. But beware: the horizon line will look broken in the corner between the walls except when the viewer's eye level is at the exact same height as the horizon line. Since you must expect viewers of different height, the problem spot should simply be obscured by a (painted) plant, palm tree, column, or other architectural element. Another solution is a folding screen (figure 31) with a portable ocean that continues

33
Colorful birds enliven the area of the sky and
define what is near. Their color connects the warm
foreground with the green of the middle ground.

34
Depth: This painting employs diverse techniques to
represent the third dimension in a painterly
manner.

3. *High-contrast light reflections and cast shadows.* The railing casts a shadow on the stone floor. The dark line can only be interpreted as a shadow, and the illusion of three-dimensionality arises. The same is true for the white highlights on the metal bars on the far edge of the floor. The railing seems to be much closer than the trees because its bright highlights create a distance rich in contrasts to the picture's middle ground.

4. *Nearby colors appear warmer and more intense.* Choosing warm and bright colors for objects in the foreground makes use of this effect. The darker the doorframe, the stronger the tunnel effect. It suggests that the foreground of the picture lies in shadow, and that the viewer has to pass through the frame to arrive at the light. The middle ground is dominated by "neutral" green, the background by a cool blue. The more blue, the wider the space. Glazed in subtle transitions toward turquoise near the horizon and ultramarine near the zenith, the sky appears to curve like a dome!

35

Creating contrasts: The middle ground was painted first, then the major sections of the balustrade were marked with tape to allow the gondolas to be positioned so that they would still be recognizable when the balustrade was completed.

36

Each part of the balustrade is stenciled and defined in grisaille. How much depth would be lost if the balustrade were replaced by a little brick wall along the shore?

5. *Different layers are aligned.* Closest is the layer containing the curtain and the door arch, next come the two columns, the railing, the green trees, the islands, and the far distance. The layers appear vertical to the direction of the viewer's gaze; there are no perspective distortions in width or breadth. Depth is created not only by diminishing size, but mainly through contrasts in color and brightness that separate the layers from each other. That is why we often find railings, gates, and other borders in murals. Their

rhythmical arrangement and the many views they create define middle and foreground as much as they create architectural space.

The railing in figures 35 and 36 is an example. The balustrade is completely in the foreground. Its presumed location is identical to the plane of the wall. Thus, it becomes possible that the actual floor seems to continue "behind" the balustrade, even though it is actually bordered by a tile edge on the wall—a common problem. This edge is incorporated into the painted balustrade as

a "real" base and is no longer perceived as a border of the floor. The floor continues all the way to the harbor wall, and the balustrade seems to cast a soft shadow on it! The light–dark contrast between balustrade and floor is repeated at the transition to the water's edge. A light edging stone was "laid" there to heighten the contrast with the dark blue of the water. Multiple layers are created.

6. *The far distance dissolves in a pale mist and mountains turn blue:* lines soften with distance, sharpen towards the foreground.

Figure 37 shows another example. Without the precisely rendered birds, the cloudy sky would not seem quite so removed. A space opens up between birds and clouds, created by the contrast of crisp lines and diffuse tonal transitions.

37
Graphic and painterly elements: their contrast heightens the illusion of depth.

Sky blue

The sky is everywhere, and there is no limit to the colorful phenomena it displays. But the illusionistic painter is only marginally interested in ground fog, thunderclouds, rain showers, or lunar eclipses. The trompe l'oeil painter specializes in fair-weather clouds, the kind that float through a sky that is forever blue.

Sky blue is immaterial, and the gloriously blue heaven is not an object but an apparition. It is easier to represent the ephemeral character of light through the use of glazes rather than opaque paints. There is a difference between a light blue that has been applied in one opaque layer and one that has been built up of several layers of glazes over a brilliantly white ground. The results may have the same tonal value, but they will reflect light differently. A glazed sky appears immaterial, even less graspable than a sky painted, sprayed, or rolled in opaque pastel blue. Glazing technique veils the ground, and with it the position of the image in space. It makes it difficult to judge exactly where the wall is located, and that helps the illusionistic painter to obscure the border between real and imagined.

Multiple layers of glaze are also ideal for the creation of subtle gradations and nuances between the horizon and the zenith. The general rule is: blue expands space, a gradient warps space. The "arch" of the sky appears in darker, clearer blues near the zenith (the upper parts of murals), and in foggier, lighter tones towards the horizon.

38 (page 29)
Detail of figure 41, page 32.

39
The sky is painted first in graduated shades and in several layers; opaque clouds are added last. To apply the glaze evenly, thin and mix the paints with a glazing medium (thickener plus retardant). The ground should not be very absorbent.

As more layers are applied in areas near the zenith than in areas near the horizon, the colors deepen, darken, and intensify automatically. To apply a glaze the paint must first be mixed with water and a glazing medium or paint retarder. The layer beneath should not be very absorbent, so that the paint can be applied swiftly without streaking.

Blue can be used to create a visionary sense of space, while clouds can be almost as dense as objects, and their representation is subject to the laws of three-dimensional space and geometric perspective. The clouds in figure 39 were painted over the glazed sky, and the atmospheric colors of the sky contrast with the whites and shadowy grays of the cloud bodies to make them substantial and voluminous. The painting becomes even more interesting if you show several types of clouds expressing lightness, movement, and depth.

Cloud shapes

Clouds are classified according to their height, the distance from their underside to the surface of the ocean. There are three major families of clouds: high clouds, about 4 to 8 miles (6 to 13 km) high; medium-height clouds, 1¼ to 4⅓ miles (2 to 7 km) high, and low clouds. A fourth family comprises clouds that stretch through all layers. Within the families, analogous to the

40
Beach chairs on the island of Sylt. The parallel
bands of cirrus clouds give the painting a strong
depth effect.

41
Boat dock on Mauritius. Here, too, a strong
perspective effect is created. The landing leads
directly toward the vanishing point on the horizon.
The impressive space is created by geometric
arrangements of cumulus formations and a wide-
angle view.

42
High-level clouds (cirrocumulus), glazed over the
sky and spread gently with a blending brush.

4

43
Diffused layers of clouds calms the color composition and softens the cast shadows.

44
Mixed clouds: a fascinating play of formation, arrangement, condensing, and dissolution.

45
Even though cumulus clouds can cast shadows onto other clouds or the landscape below, they cannot really be considered objects. They represent conditions in the atmosphere and they are in constant flux. Their white color comes from the diffusion of light across the entire spectrum. Thicker clouds can look dark gray if viewed directly from below, but this color, like the white, is a fleeting appearance and not a permanent attribute.

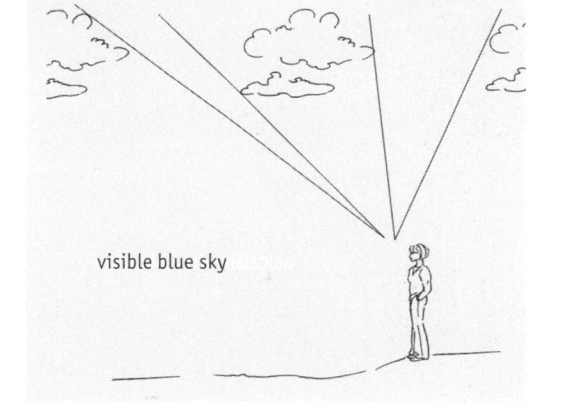

46, 47

Two important aspects of painting cumulus formations are the condensation height (distance from the bottom of the cloud to the ground) and the distance between clouds. The condensation level creates a continuous plane that can be used as part of a perspective composition to create depth in the painting. In addition, it is good to remember that in an evenly clouded sky it always appears as though there are fewer clouds directly overhead and more in the distance. For the same reason the sky appears predominantly blue at the zenith, even if the cloud cover is even across the sky. The sketch explains this phenomenon and demonstrates why a painted sky mural should always show denser clouds near the edges of the ceiling and almost none in the middle.

classification system of plants and animals, are subgroups, named for their type of formation. Stratus (Latin for "layer") clouds appear at all heights in stable atmosphere.

Puffy cumulus (Latin for "heap") clouds appear in unstable atmosphere, and cirrus (Latin for "wisp of hair") clouds form at high altitudes from water vapor that freezes directly, without ever taking liquid form. All other clouds consist of condensed water vapor or tiny frozen droplets. There are ten more groups and yet more subdivisions, but we will only discuss those that are important for light and cheerful paintings.

Veil-like cirrus clouds are painted by the sky itself with a pure white glaze of ice crystals thinned by the wind. They drift high across the sky at great speed, like ribbons or strands of hair. They often announce a change in weather. Their typical feathery formation appears when the tail follows the head at a lower altitude and lower speed. It is easy to paint such forms. Cirrus clouds have no form shadows: do not use grays or purples in them, but layer them in blue glazes to create depth as needed. They will appear transparent and fade into the background. Their soft shapes conform to Leonardo da Vinci's ideal of *sfumato*—smoky or foggy colors, achieved by adding white, which help to define depth in the painting.

Cirrus clouds can appear in almost parallel ribbons and give much depth to a painting because the entire formation can seem to end in one common vanishing point (see figures 27, page 19, and 40, page 31).

High cirrocumulus clouds appear as small white specks, thin flakes, or fuzzy balls and they often form in patterns or rows (figure 42, page 33). In contrast to altocumulus, their underside has no shadow and is pure white. Figure 41 (page 32) shows altocumulus and cirrocumulus formations. Cirrostratus, high layered clouds, are of little interest to the illusionistic painter since they cover the blue sky in a thin white streaky veil or in white fog.

The weather will change. Cirrostratus interest is indirect, because the presence of these clouds diffuses the light and lightens cast shadows, which are not usually shown in a totally realistic manner in large murals, but only suggested where they are useful (figure 43, page 34).

At medium height, cirrus or cumulus clouds can develop, often as puffy altocumulus in layers. Many small cloud puffs form a relatively flat carpet with a bumpy or irregularly structured surface. Between the woolly puffs flecks of blue sky can be seen. Altocumulus is related to cirrocumulus, only these clouds are larger and darker,

48

Cumulus humilis, mediocris, and congestus (Latin for "crowded') in sequential development. Additional small and dark cloud segments and cirrostratus with lots of blue sky in the background: a very picturesque ensemble.

Low to mid-height vertical cloud formations fascinate by the fleeting balance of form and substance. High cirrus clouds appear as signs in the sky, hurriedly painted and without any material essence. Low stratocumulus, on the other hand, have no clear contours and develop into rain clouds. Form or shape is not important and the heavy material aspect becomes dominant. Cumulus humilis and mediocris (the quintessential clouds) give us both extremes: voluminous, with a clearly formed body, shadows and light absorption, and at the same time clear contours and ever-changing and fraying shapes on the upper edges. These shapes invite interpretation as images or symbols: "This one looks like a . . . "

49

Dissolving vertical clouds. Thermal convection is illustrated in this image. Shreds of clouds are dancing in the sky, following an intense choreography, and disappear seconds later.

50

Every large sky mural should follow a preliminary chalk sketch on the wall or on a canvas. Drawings, photos, or patterns are essential for a convincing design of cloud shapes and their distribution in the picture. The necessary colors are mixed beforehand in sufficient quantities: three shades of blue, one or two grays, and white. During the work these basic colors are continually mixed and blended with each other.

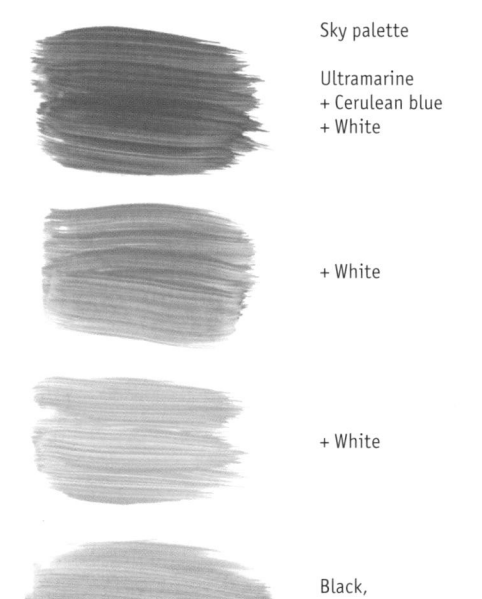

Sky palette

Ultramarine
+ Cerulean blue
+ White

+ White

+ White

Black,
Deep violet
+ White

51

Start with light colors and the lower part. The clouds near the horizon are small and grouped in horizontal formations. Avoid strong contrasts at this stage of the work: details and denser areas will develop later. When one area of the painting is perfected prematurely, the total effect and unity of the painting often suffers as a result.

52

Paint areas of cirrus clouds wet-on-wet and use blue and white paint simultaneously. Apply the paint with a bristle brush. When the brush is "dry," continue to paint and blend the different field of colors into smooth transitions.

53

Use darker shades toward the upper edge of the painting, but reserve the darkest blues or grays for the last layer. Create a regular and smooth progression from lighter to darker clouds. Intense acrylic colors applied as glazes or too much paint on a brush will invariably result in streaks and should be avoided.

54

Leave the clouds white. Details like shading and edges will be added later in shades of blue, gray, and white. Compared to figure 53, the clouds here appear smaller and more differentiated in the expanded blue sky, the blue areas quieter. At this stage the sizes and shapes of the clouds can be fine-tuned. Different color nuances are created by applying paint in thin layers. The sky is much more than a simple expanse of blue, but shows richly varied and subtle hues.

55
The voluminous bodies of clouds are defined with grays and whites. Before the work begins you must decide from which side the light falls so that shadows and gleaming highlights on the clouds are applied consistently. Gray should be used sparingly in the upper part of the painting to avoid any association with rain clouds.

56
The gray color for this cloud was mixed from black, white, and a touch of violet with sky blue, which makes the lower part of the clouds retreat optically. White tips are added last. Interior acrylic paints can be used for this purpose.

opaque and tinted gray. Blue glazes are of limited usefulness here because altocumulus clouds are too close to the observer to fade into the blue distance, but geometric shapes can be used to create depth if you render the clearly delineated shapes in perspective foreshortening. We won't deal with the medium-high rain-bringing layers of altostratus clouds that appear like dark brews, or with the vertical nimbostratus rain clouds.

Layered clouds in the lowest altitudes are stratocumulus—flat forms that look like tousled cotton puffs, which arise through thermal processes like convection, but not in the typical cauliflower shape. Such layers can be shown in the far distance, above the horizon. Clouds in the distance are hard to distinguish; they might be cumulus or stratocumulus layers several square miles in size, but because of their low density the sky can show through many holes.

57
This figure shows the wide variety of cloud shapes that are possible in an illusionistic sky painting. A vertical formation in a "broccoli" shape rises from the streaky carpet of cumulus clouds. At the same level but "closer" to the viewer, another cloud ensemble floats in mid-air on the right: shadowed at the bottom, illuminated by the sun at the top, well balanced in volume and with fuzzy edges. The frayed upper section suggests a slight upwards motion. The clouds at the upper edge of the painting seem to float or drift almost directly above the viewer's head. Transparent fields of cirrus clouds are blown about in distant heights. Because the voluminously modeled rising clouds are shown in front of transparent veils, three-dimensional space is created and appears very credible.

58
Depending on one's personal tastes and specific uses of the painting, the realistic representation of the sky can be combined with other elements such as birds or tree tops seen from below. Here we transferred some of Raphael's putti onto the sky. A white underpainting makes the colors more luminous.

The ideal cumulus sky

Cumulus humilis (Latin for "humble") is the favorite cloud, not just of illusionistic painters. On a summer day in temperate zones this fair-weather cloud can dissolve as quickly as it forms. It brings no precipitation and a flat, gray, and almost horizontal base and a rounded, slightly puffy and well-defined upper part. The base is usually longer than the height of the cloud (figure 45, page 35). Alternatively, there is the cumulus mediocris (Latin for "medium") which has a smaller base-to-height ratio compared to the cumulus humilis. Mediocris is another rain-free cloud well liked by painters and illustrators and it is commonly considered the very model of a fair-weather cloud (figures 46–48, pages 35 and 36) so long as it does not develop into a cauliflower-shaped cumulonimbus, the thunder-cloud.

High winds rip these clouds into shreds called cumulus fractus (Latin for "broken") and drive them across the sky at great speed and in constantly changing shapes (figure 49, page 37).

59
A painted sky at three stages. This painting is less complex than the previous example and shows an overview of the basic approach.

These clouds have ragged edges, no defined base, and no contoured puffs. The overhead veil-like ragged fractus forms are not as dark as the undersides of humilis or mediocris clouds.

It is best to show stratocumulus in the distance, cumulus humilis in the mid-layer of the sky, and cumulus fractus near the zenith. This distribution supports in an ideal manner all efforts to create a perspective grid, as explained earlier.

5 The Sea

The sea has many facets. Here we are dealing with the ones that create a carefree and sunny impression in an illusionistic painting. Everybody likes the sea when it glitters in the sun, when the water is clear near the shore and deep blue in the distance. Close to the beach we usually see light waves with white crests. If we look at the ocean from an elevated position on a calm day, the situation will be reversed: The water near us shows bright colors and fades toward the horizon. The painter is interested in optical phenomena like the reflection and diffusion of light in the water and on its surface (figures 61–64) as well as the surf. How do waves arise, break, and wash over the beach (figures 65–68)?

Using a glazing technique to paint light reflections and ripples in several layers makes sense for a medium that is as alive, fluctuating, and transparent as water. How could transparency be represented if not through transparent layers? The light that penetrates the layers of glaze and is reflected by the white underpainting mimics the light that illuminates the sea and is reflected by the ocean floor. Figures 69–82 show different possibilities. Figures 83–96 show how to paint the surf realistically.

61

The sun stands high in front of the viewer. The shadow sides of the ripples are dark blue or dark turquoise; their sides facing the sun are lighter. Intermittently there are areas of strong light reflections that appear like a white veil (the angle of the incident light equals that of the reflected light, implying that the sun stands high). In the foreground the sand can be seen through the transparent, turquoise clear water. The water in the foreground is bright because the light is reflected by the light-colored bottom underneath. The shade of turquoise comes from the presence of microorganisms that reflect green light (as do green terrestrial plants). Where the water is deep and far away we see mostly opaque dark blues.

62

Open water seen from a boat. The sun is high above the viewer. The reflections appear as glittering sparkles. The wave in the foreground is not white-capped—its white "crown" is caused by light reflections on the moving waters at the crest. The blue of the water results from light refraction, an effect that also takes place in the atmosphere and produces "sky blue." The ocean bottom reflects only a small amount of light; thus, the overall color is relatively dark, and it would be darker yet if the sun stood low. A smaller angle of incident light lets less light penetrate the surface and more of the light is reflected from it.

63

Beach at noon: The sun stands high; a lot of light enters the water and makes it look intensely blue. The damp areas on the beach reflect the blue sky, but this effect is visible only if the viewer sees the scene from the side and not from directly above.

64

Beach in evening light: The water appears blue-black, hidden by a golden veil of light. The sunlight comes in at a low angle; most of it is reflected, and the damp beach turns into an image of the evening sky.

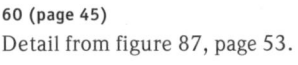

60 (page 45)
Detail from figure 87, page 53.

65

A wave is illuminated by evening light; churned up sand makes it appear in a light olive green. The foam of the breaking crest lies in the wave's own shadow, and its white coloration is veiled in cool blues. The foam patterns on the wave's leeward side are barely discernible because light is shining through them.

66

Here the sun is at the viewer's back. The wave's foam glows in brilliant white, while its body appears green-black because very little light enters. The foam pattern on the leeward side becomes very pronounced.

67

This picture shows all the stages of the surf, which originates when ocean waves reach the shore. In the open sea the water masses remain largely stationary, oscillating in circular motion. This motion of the water "particles" becomes visible as crests and troughs but also takes place invisibly, below the surface. In shallow waters near the shore the oscillation is interrupted when the depth of the water is less than half a wavelength (a wavelength is the distance between two waves). The lower part of the wave slows down, and the distance between the waves decreases, while the crests grow taller and steeper until they break. For the painter the visible elements are most important. The arrows in the picture indicate the direction of the water movement.

68

Reflection and refraction of light as the water droplets of the crest create multiple light effects. In the collapsing wave water and air mix and create opaque white foam. Depending upon the force of the wind and the clarity of the water, this foam can be carried onto the beach and remain there briefly. On the beach water moves in two opposite directions: it washes up the beach in a swash and drains in the backwash.

69

To create a glittering summer sea we start with an underpainting in a gradation of white near the horizon, turquoise blue below, then ultramarine. All colors are applied with great care, beginning with the lightest shade.

70

Before any painting can be done, the palette has to be prepared, and all colors must be mixed in sufficient quantities. Their consistency should be watery so the color can flow from the brush freely. In this study we only used turquoise and aquamarine, mixed with white. On the left are the colors for the underpainting; on the right, the palette for the wave strokes.

71, 72

The use of a mahlstick, bridge, or ruler is helpful to achieve a consistently horizontal orientation of brushstrokes. Work with thin brushes near the horizon line, with thicker ones near the bottom of the painting—this way the waves in the background appear farther away. The image is built up in many layers and with increasingly darker tones. Finally, white highlights make the water glitter.

The brushstrokes should not be applied too uniformly. Variations in water depth, formations on the ocean floor, wind gusts—all have visible effect on the sensitive surface of the sea. Around the horizon a white glaze was applied as a finishing touch. The horizon line fades into the distance; sea and sky seem to merge.

73

Palette of colors for water and beach: turquoise and ultramarine, and a touch of each mixed with white. Warm and cool browns (raw umber plus ochre and raw umber plus black) are also mixed with white in gradations.

74

For this truly multilayered project we did not start with the sea but with the beach and the sea bottom. Only some areas in the front remain white where the water will later shine brightly, unbroken by the beige of the ground beneath. The stones are indicated with darker shades of brown and black, larger formations in the front, narrow strips and much lighter towards the back.

75

The water is "filled in." A scumble glaze is prepared from retardants and thickeners and applied in irregular strips, dense in the front and lighter in the back. In accordance with perspective diminution, larger brushes and brushstrokes are used in front, smaller brushes and strokes in back.

76

After the paint has dried briefly, it can be scumbled—partially removed by rubbing a damp rag or brush in wavelike motions over parts of the painting. Avoid streaking! The result will be lighter areas that will later look like light reflections even if they are glazed again later.

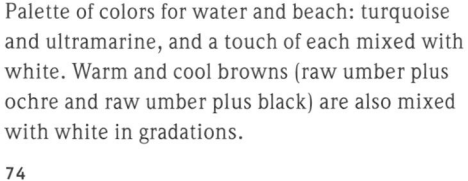

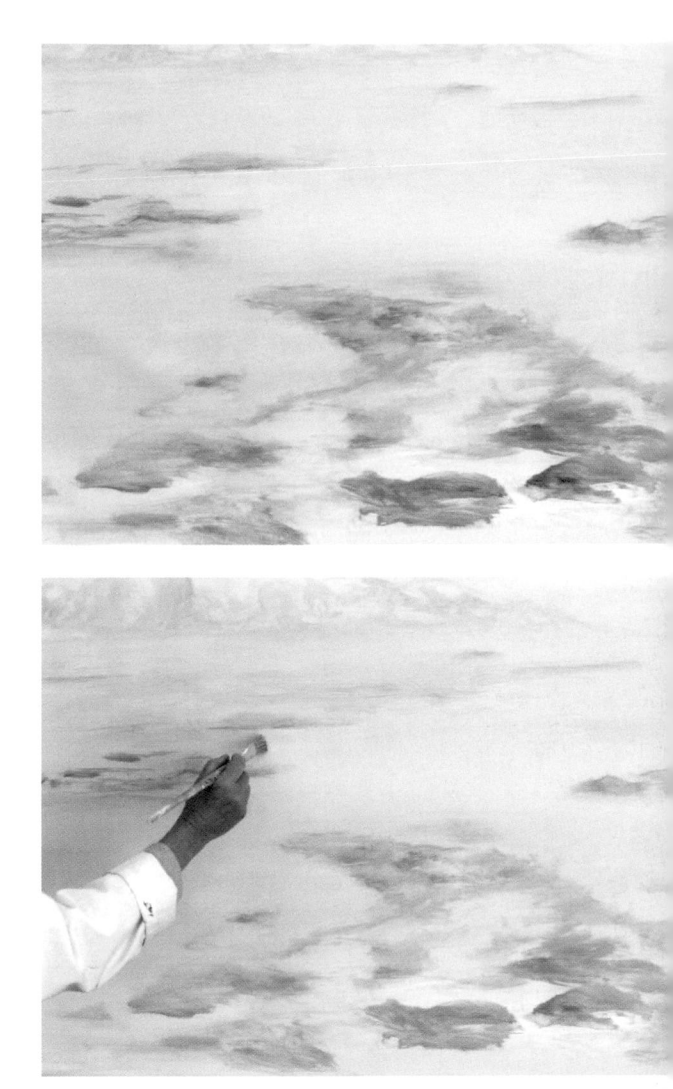

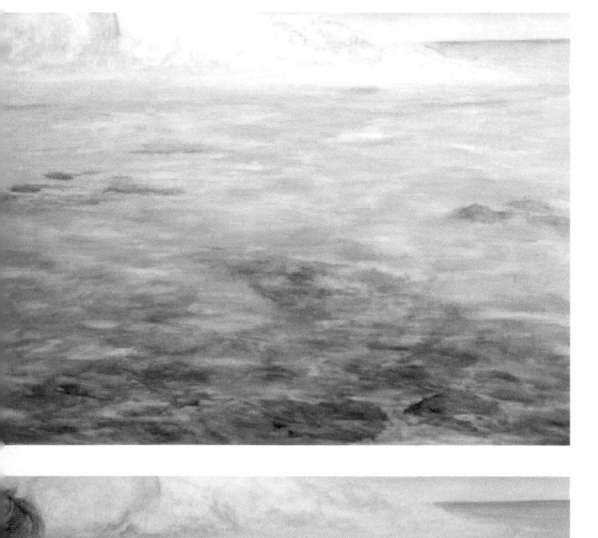

77

To deepen the color, a second layer of turquoise and light blue is applied; composition and brightness can be fine-tuned in this step. The area near the bottom may need several layers to reach the desired intensity. The light reflections that have been left white in the first layer should be painted with great care. The color of the stones can be enhanced with a dark blue; their shapes should not be painted as outlines but as if cutting them into slices. If brushstrokes break the contours of the stones, it will create the illusion of looking at them through moving water.

78

For the next layer a mix of turquoise-blue, and Payne's gray (blue-black) is applied as transparent glaze in areas of shadow and over dark stones. These streaky shadows, subordinated to the light reflections, should only be used in areas of low light—in this case on the left sides of the rocks. Additional light spots can be painted with white. For light reflections in the distance, the white paint is mixed with a trace of turquoise or blue.

79

As a finishing touch, the part of the island that is above water can be defined further to balance color saturations and areas of light and dark.

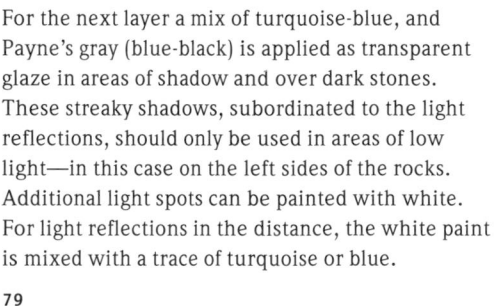

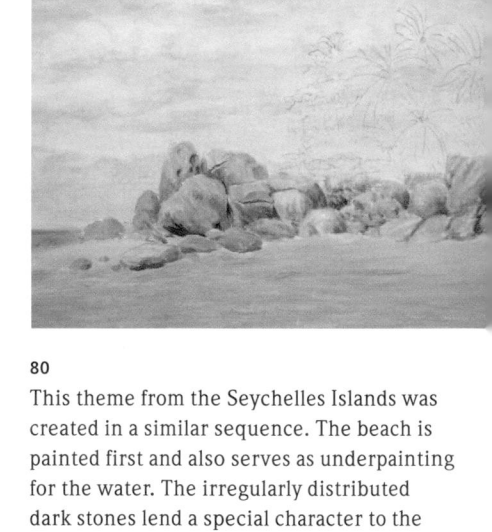

80

This theme from the Seychelles Islands was created in a similar sequence. The beach is painted first and also serves as underpainting for the water. The irregularly distributed dark stones lend a special character to the sea.

81

Water and land are painted simultaneously. The turquoise sea splashes all the way to the rocks. While the light beige of the rocks requires a white underpainting, the sketch of the vegetation remains an outline. Darker and opaque shades of green can be applied over the color of the sky.

82

An island born of desire. Don't interfere with the
dreamlike character of the image by using crisp
outlines or too many details, and the island will
rise from the transparent sea like an apparition.

Ultramarine +
Cerulean blue +
Phthalo blue
+ White + Payne's gray   + White   + Perma-   + Ochre   + Cerulean   + Turquoise   Ultramarine + White
                                            nent   + White   blue   + Payne's gray
                                            green   + White

83

Step-by-step surf: Paint the sky first and put a strip of masking tape exactly above the horizon line. For the ocean, start by painting the beach in light beige fading into white for the lower third of the painting. Next comes a darker beige that already shows the shape of the water splashing onto the shore. This darker beige represents the area of wet sand; the light beige is the dry sand. Finally the water: Start near the horizon with the darkest shades and apply the paint only in horizontal streaks. No vertical or rounded brushstrokes here!

As you gradually move toward medium-light areas, leave out occasional white strips that will later be white foam crests. A dark blue contour along the lower edges of these white areas will create images of waves as if by magic!

A wider strip of white is left free for the surf; in front of it shades of blue and turquoise become increasingly transparent toward the bottom of the painting. Give the surf a light greenish yellow in the upper part where the sun shines through, and apply it in lightly rounded brushstrokes. The lower part of the wave is bluish green, since it lies in shadow and is darker than the ocean in front of it. Opaquely painted foam can later hide breaks in the color transitions. In this painting the foamy areas were left white from the beginning.

84

The next layer is also painted from back to front; brightness and the amount of green in the mix increase as you go. Use only thin brushes near the horizon! Formerly white areas are now glazed in

blue and look like light reflections. The breaking crest of the wave (formerly the windward side of it) gets a yellowish green structure, somewhat darker than the green leeward side, through which the sunlight can be seen. The crashing masses of water mirror the sinuous rising of the trough in the opposite direction; both motions together describe an oval. Intensify the water in front of the wave with blue and turquoise glazes.

85

Foam crests are applied in opaque white, their shadows in gray mixed from white and a touch of black or Payne's gray. Avoid mechanical movements; instead, apply the paint in dots, short lines, or with a sponge. As always, deepen structures with darker shades.

86

Here is a palette of sea colors as you could find them in the North Sea or the European coasts of the Atlantic. You will not find Caribbean turquoise here! The water is full of floating particles that give it a jade-green color; even the darker blues have a hint of green in them.

87

In painting the foam that waves leave behind on the beach, avoid parallel lines and repetitive shapes! Finally, paint the netlike patterns of foam on the wave itself with a finer brush than was used for the spidery lines in the foreground. To suggest the dampness of the sand immediately in front of an incoming wave, add a bluish glaze, which will look like a diffused mirror image of the sky.

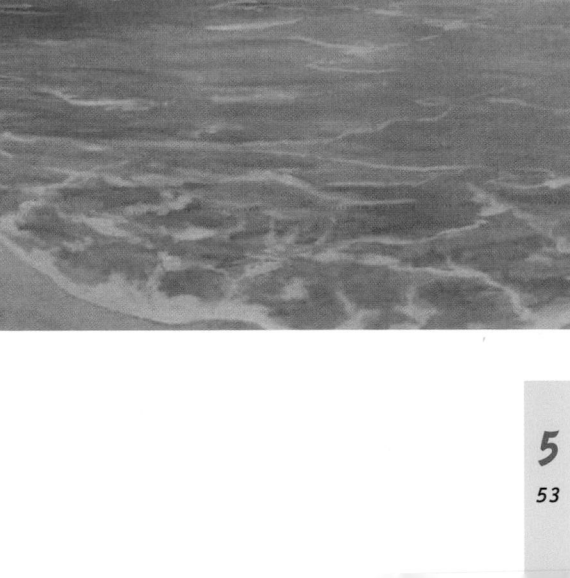

88

A second example for this technique. The color scheme lies between a Caribbean (figure 93, page 58) and a northern palette and is universally applicable. The illustration shows the second stage of painting—the wave is clearly defined, the colors are heightened, and some contours of rocks are recognizable on the beach.

89

While the white foam in the previous painting was the white ground itself, additional white paint was used here, and together with some gray in the shadows, it creates three-dimensionality. There are netlike patterns in the foreground, and the white-capped crest casts a shadow on the sand below the surface.

90

This detail shows that foam and spray can take many different forms: blown about by the wind, a seething white broth, dancing at the top of the wave. Illuminated from behind, a wave appears moving and alive; where it is breaking, the sunlight hits the top, and the painter can represent the strong reflections to accentuate the rounded forms. The strands of foam lifted by the rising waves can be shown in the same way.

91

Panoramic view with sky and flock of seagulls. The waves and the birds' flight move in opposite directions, which gives dynamic strength to the painting. The foam pattern on the beach can be seen only on the right side because the beach rises slightly toward the left. A fourth direction of motion is indicated by the clouds. The topics of sea and sky are superbly suited to visualize dynamic movement. Such a mural creates not only the feeling of wide open space but of lightness, liveliness, and motion into the distance.

92
The most important steps in the "three-stage picture."

Ocean palette

Turquoise | Permanent green + Touch of white | + More white | Even more white | More white | Ultramarine + Cerulean blue + Touch of Phthalo green + Touch of white

93
Caribbean palette. These colors were used for the beach party painting (figure 22, page 16). Figure 96 shows a detail.

94
As the wave laps onto the beach, it leaves some foam behind: blue "dampness" is applied beneath the white of the wave's edge.

95
Blue and blue-gray dots are painted on the white foam areas and later heightened with white: a small band of foam appears.

96
A well-rendered transition between beach and water.

6 *Special Light Conditions*

97
Evening sky over Paris: An impressive and quite dramatic photograph, but it would be difficult to turn it into a mural. It is much too gray and much too dense! It is, however, possible to make use of some of the elements: (1) The silhouette of the houses can be used as a foreground that effectively suggests depth and an elevated point of view. (2) The light source just outside the edge of the picture sets the scene for a dramatic view of moving clouds in the front. (3) The cloud shapes in the background and their geometric structure create depth and tension between background and foreground.

98
The evening sky in this trompe l'oeil painting fits the function of the room. It expands the bedroom visually and creates a feeling of peace and relaxation because of the large area of blue sky that serves as background for the complex composition of clouds. In contrast to the actual sky on which it was modeled, the colors of the painted clouds are subdued and the color of the sky itself is more intense. Without such freedom the mural might feel oppressive to the viewer and appear psychologically restricting rather than liberating over a period of time. The illusionistic painter works from nature, but does not copy it. Photographs serve as guidelines for the composition and structure of a natural setting, but it is never the purpose of the painting simply to reproduce a photograph.

Certain light situations simply cannot be painted without producing kitsch. We call a picture kitschy if the viewer has no freedom to form an individual impression—that is to say that the message of the painting is predetermined as a sort of emotional instant-effect. In a way this applies to all illusion-istic paintings, since they aim to achieve particular effects like the apparent enlargement of a room, or present a certain subject in a way that creates a distinct emotional setting. A fairly neutral painting will be least restrictive to the viewer. It is almost impossible to represent sunsets in this way, since they touch most people emotionally. Murals of sunsets also fulfill a second criterion for kitsch: banal simplification. The energy-filled glow of the sinking sun changes from second to second; what

does it have to do with material pigments permanently adhered to a wall? Is there any connection left between the grand experience of the moment under the open sky and the colorful decor of an interior space? And one more question needs to be answered: Are the grand motifs chosen by a painter too much for the simple purpose of a picture? Or is the purpose—to move or awe the viewer—too much for the technical skills of the artist?

100
Color palette used for painting figure 102. The color samples seem opaque, but in the painting the colors were applied as glazes, which makes them appear lighter and more transparent than on the palette.

101
Answers to these questions have to be formulated according to the specific circumstances of the painting job at hand. As a general rule it can be said that just as a moonlit evening sky is appropriate for bedrooms (figure 98), sunsets could be used for rooms one uses for brief periods only during evening hours. In our example we applied

large areas of color in gradations from blue-violet and pastel pink to shades of yellow. They are lightest near the setting sun. To avoid streaking, the colors were applied in multiple layers.

102
The motifs in the foreground are shown as warm silhouettes on the wall; careful shading is very important. The sail of the catamaran is slightly transparent; the trunks of the palm trees are shaped by barely visible white highlights. The smaller palm trees in the background have less clearly defined outlines to create an impression of depth.

103
Flock of seagulls in an evening sky (photograph).

104
The ocean is shown in gradations of silvery turquoise veiled in gray. The atmosphere is reminiscent of the birds in figure 103. The wave structures are indicated with light and airy brushstrokes—a calligraphy of waves.

105
The stylized approach and the reduction of the motifs to the most basic elements create a modern, almost surreal impression. The movement of the waves and the flock of birds above the low horizon are highly decorative.

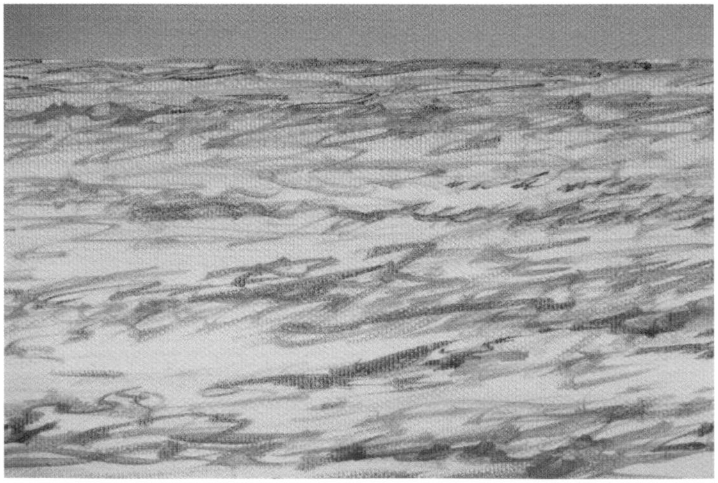

106

Evening at the seaside after a light monsoon rain in Sri Lanka. The sun is hidden behind tattered clouds, the atmosphere is diffusely illuminated, and glistening light envelops the water. The coloration is subtle and harmonized because the palette consists of only three colors: red, yellow, and blue.

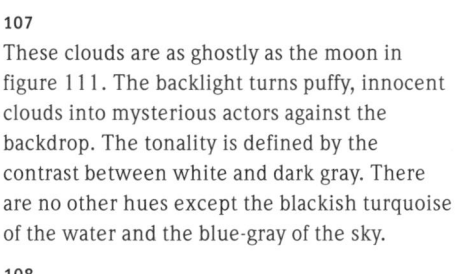

107
These clouds are as ghostly as the moon in figure 111. The backlight turns puffy, innocent clouds into mysterious actors against the backdrop. The tonality is defined by the contrast between white and dark gray. There are no other hues except the blackish turquoise of the water and the blue-gray of the sky.

108
For this night sky we mixed ultramarine blue with Payne's gray and white. The clouds are painted over a white ground for better contrast with the sky. It is best to apply this ground in an irregular fashion, opaque and transparent in different places, and with fuzzy edges.

109
The second layer of clouds is painted with ochre, gray, and white. The paint is daubed on and spread with a rag immediately afterward to form soft or slightly streaked edges. The effect is that of pale moonlight.

110
Blue-gray is applied with a soft rag and creates the appearance of diffuse light. The wiping motion can result in pleasing structures that suggest blurry cloud edges and shadows.

111
As a final touch, highlights are added.

112

View from an airplane between two cloud layers. Such spectacular sunsets could inspire a painter to create murals that are "out of this world," far from everyday reality. No viewer would believe that a scene like this could exist daily somewhere in the atmosphere. And if it did happen, who would be there to see it?

113

This somewhat less dramatic backlit view is poetical because of its color scheme. The geometrically arranged cloud banks lead the eye towards a vanishing point not far from the sun. What winged creature floats over the waters at the top right?

Wall or ceiling?

114

Ceiling murals are not just for grand mansions. In houses with relatively low ceilings or small and badly proportioned rooms, a sky painted on a ceiling can do wonders. The artist has a choice of painting directly on the ceiling or on canvas or paper to be glued in place later. In rooms with many corners, rooms with many spotlights in the ceiling, or rooms where there are other unfavorable conditions, we suggest that large sky paintings be executed on location—that is, painted directly onto the ceiling. Working overhead is very tiring; a rolling scaffold that reaches close to the ceiling makes the work easier, especially if it allows you to paint from an almost reclined position. Check ceiling murals from the floor periodically to ensure that the desired appearance of depth is being created. It is difficult to judge from up close while painting.

115

If the dimensions are manageable, many artists who are comfortable with the gluing process prefer to work on movable supports. Paintings on paper or canvas do not necessarily require a completely smooth ground: the fabric can even out minor irregularities. The stabilization of the ceiling surface and the prevention of cracks is a problem that should not be underestimated. When painting directly onto the ceiling, you may have to adhere paper or fabric before painting, to prevent cracks. Another issue is the fact that images overhead look different than when they are on a wall. Thus, it is difficult to gauge the effect of a painting on the horizontal ceiling while it is hanging on a vertical wall. The only solution is to hold up a good copy or photograph of each stage of the work and look at it from below. The illustrations in this chapter should also be viewed this way.

Summer sky with light clouds

116

Without a design it is difficult to maintain an overview of the work. The composition has to be clear from the beginning and outlines are transferred to the painting surface in chalk. The next step is a light foundation painting in pale blue and white. This first layer defines the placement of the basic shapes, but not yet the details. The thin, transparent paint is applied in criss-cross strokes and blended wet-on-wet. Use the paint sparingly and work the brushes hard!

117

The blue is darkest in the middle of the ceiling. Don't destroy the depth effect of the color by obscuring the center with clouds. Near the edges of the picture, the clouds are grouped in irregular, accidental forms, some large, others small.

118

The imaginary sun is shining from the top left. A soft shade of ochre suggests that the sun stands low. The clouds are illuminated from the side accordingly: they are bright on the right side, shadowy on the left. The shadows are painted in gray with a touch of violet. They should not get too dark, or they will lose the appearance of lightness.

119

The large cloud shapes in figure 118 have already been worked out in minute detail. A group of puffy clouds drifts away from the shape at the right edge of the picture. The clouds drift in the shadow of their "mother cloud." In some other places the clouds have been dissolved, frayed, and reduced in size to give more room to the blue of the sky. The application of highlights gives the imaginary sun an almost dramatic presence.

Zenith perspective

120

An even stronger effect of depth can be achieved if geometric perspective is added to the suggestive force of the color blue. What central perspective is for a wall mural, zenith perspective is for the ceiling mural: the central vanishing point lies in the middle of the painting. In this painting, however, it has been moved slightly along the middle line, which makes the composition more pleasant: the viewer is not required to stand in the middle of the room to view the ceiling.

With such a construction, painting should not begin until every last line has been clarified! It is incomparably more difficult to construct lines on a wall or a ceiling than on a piece of paper on a desktop, not to mention making corrections. Crisp edges can be achieved with the help of masking tape.

121

Architectural paintings are also developed in layers. All elements have to be matched to each other if a realistic light-and-shadow effect is desired. This is most likely to succeed if painting progresses evenly across the entire image and you do not succumb to the temptation to "finish" one portion after another.

122

A challenge of this motif is the limited palette. An entire spectrum of cool and warm, light and dark shades of sepia brown was carefully balanced to shape the illusionary architecture out of light and shadow.

123

Perspective construction drawing for a balustrade that will be seen from below. With the help of horizontal and vertical mirror images, an entire ceiling can be designed with this rendering. The only condition is that all vanishing lines should meet at one point after the segments have been assembled.

124

At the end, the columns are slightly marbled, highlights are applied, and edges sharpened. A decorative patina and an aesthetic "ruins" look has been forgone. Perspective takes center stage and unfolds to its best advantage with "smooth" architecture.

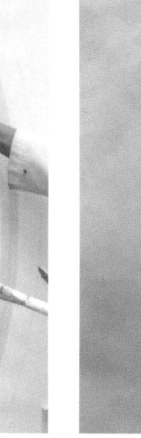

Dramatic summer sky

125

In contrast to the linear perspective of the architectural images, depth in this ceiling mural is created through color and aerial perspective. Cloud shapes are only suggested and do not distract from the filigree branches and leaves. In the first layer light blues with white are painted wet-on-wet with a lightly loaded brush using relatively dry strokes.

126

The white sections can be intensified by superimposing a touch of white paint and spreading it with a "dry" bristle brush previously used for the blue paint. Aim for soft and gentle gradations.

127

The white molding is part of the painting on canvas, later cut in a round shape and glued to the ceiling. Since plaster advances optically, it is not necessary to hide the edges of the canvas on the ceiling. The painted molding shows a different distribution of light and shadow in every segment of the circle: the imaginary light comes from the side, so the angle of the profile changes continually around the edge in reference to the direction of the light.

128

The branches are sketched in chalk and based on a photo or a drawing. Painting from memory usually leads to less-than-realistic results. The final painting is done in light browns, thicker and darker in front, lighter and more diffuse in back. Light and

129

The decorative red blossoms are daubed on with a brush. Here, too, closer and more distant elements are distinguished by more or less intense coloration. Observe carefully: Blossoms are not evenly distributed—some branches have only green leaves, others are heavily laden with red, and some are bare.

130

The composition depends on the contrast between serene sky and filigree branches. Within the branch section tension exists between leaves and blossoms, near and far. As a final touch, the clouds at the bottom are slightly intensified and shaded.

shadow can be discerned clearly on the branches in front. They are partially overlapped by a light pattern cast by the feathery leaves above. Leaves closer to the viewer are shown darker and with more precision; those in the back are lighter and more diffuse. This way the tree seems to stretch high into the sky above the viewer.

Palm tree seen from below

131
This is not a ceiling painting, but because the crown of the palm tree on the upper edge of the painting is seen almost directly from underneath, the image has been included in this chapter.

132
Motifs like this towering coconut palm are excellent subjects for ceiling murals.

133
Finely differentiated realistic paintings require detailed patterns. The outline in figure 131 was drawn from a photograph of a palm tree. Transferred onto an ink-jet or laser transparency, it can be projected onto the painting surface with an overhead projector.

134
The projector method makes drawing on the wall superfluous. When the projector is turned off, sections that have already been painted seem to float in isolation on the surface of the painting. That is because such an image is not transferred 1:1 per square inch, but is built up from the back: the most distant branches, which might even be covered by others later, are painted first, the ones in front are done later.

135
Countless shades of green are necessary for the fronds. Even if the branches in the shade are painted in dark green and those in the sun, light green, there are many variations because of the differences in local color.

136
For the shadow, Payne's gray is mixed with the color of the sand—in this case raw umber and ochre. Be careful with sienna: its reddish hue leads to unattractive graying if turquoise blue water comes in contact with the sand. The shadow is painted with loose, irregular strokes in a watery glaze. Trust your eye: the outline cannot be constructed! Using a light chalk drawing will make the job easier.

137
This symphony in green and ochre contributes much to the charm of the palm crown. The light reflections on the trunk and the tree's shadow on the beach (see figures 136, 138) intensify the perception of a sunny day.

Sky, sea, beach, a palm tree . . . less won't do;
more is not necessary to fuel the imagination.

Seas and skies look different from every spot on earth. The examples in this chapter stand for countless other possibilities of such views; they offer inspiration to those who are in search of fresh motifs beyond tired clichés.

Behind the walls

Figures 139–141 and 143 show designs for tall trompe l'oeil pictures with painted architectural frames. Such paintings measure usually 20 to 40 sq ft (2 to 4 sq m), the same size as actual doors or windows set into a wall. The style of the painting and details, such as rustic arches in a rough-hewn wall or windows without panes, for example, suggest the cultural location. All four designs share the theme of an opening through the wall and show a view of white houses. The white architecture against blue sea and sky exudes freshness and clarity. Figure 142 shows a solution that is particularly welcome in small and windowless rooms, making them appear larger and more airy. The wall is only marginally defined as a real plane in the room. Three wooden posts in the foreground support a construction with bamboo blinds. All the elements are connected by ropes. The color palette consists of only a few wood colors in the foreground and several shades of blue in the background.

Linear clarity

Clear, unadorned architecture is shown in figures 144–146 (pages 86–87). There is great simplicity in the compositions. All pictures feature places to sit down—a hammock, a chair; all invite the viewer to enjoy the view of the ocean. Figure 144 shows how to avoid the problem of a "broken" horizon. In the corner of the room (represented by the book's center fold), the horizon line is interrupted by architectural elements. The charm of figure 146 lies in its simplicity. The plain language of architectural forms stands in strong contrast to the bright and cheerful coloration. Painted plants would be redundant. The charm of figure 145 comes from the aesthetic interest of an otherwise utilitarian railing.

Its shadow, however, and its gleaming white upper edge give a special expression to the entire image. Further interest is added by the raised viewpoint of the observer who looks directly onto the chair, as well as by the use of contrasts between complementary colors and sizes of color fields.

More than palm trees and sailboats

Think of your dream beach and images of palm tree–lined shorelines are likely to surface. The word "ocean" summons up associations of white sailboats and yachts. Figures 147–150 (pages 88–89) show surprising interpretations of these themes. The traditional Sri Lankan outrigger towed ashore by fishermen offers an attractive focal point with its orange sail (figure 149).

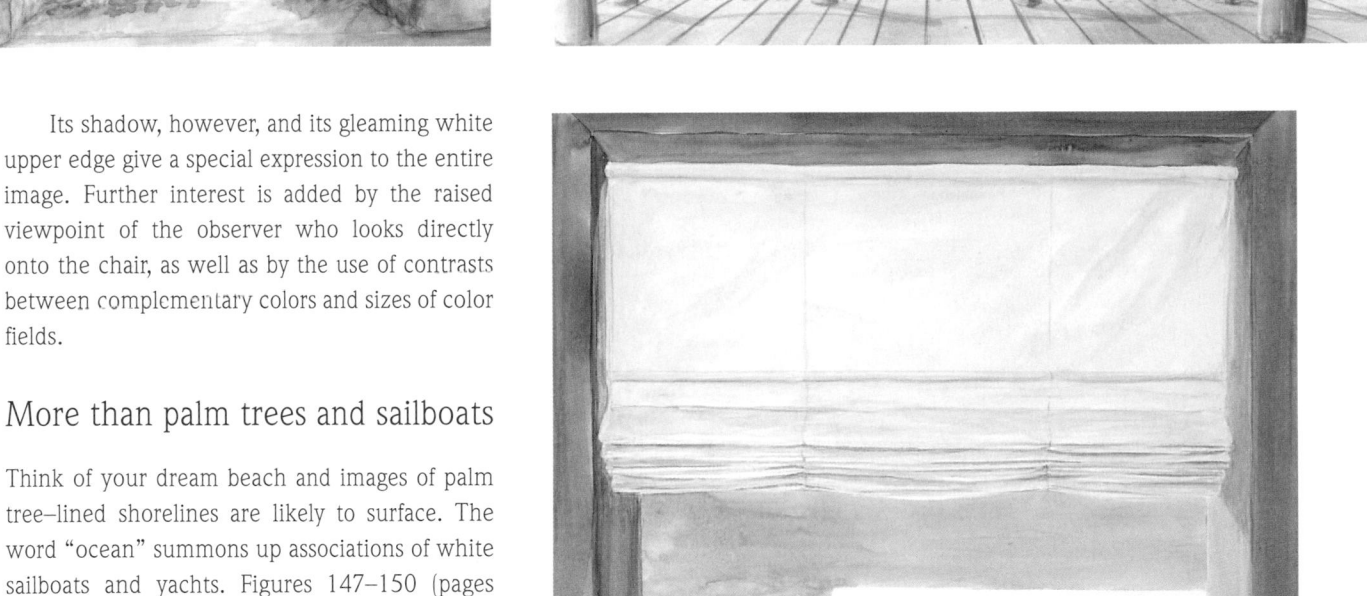

The surfer and his brightly colored gear serve a similar purpose in figure 147. In Italy picturesque pine trees grow in close proximity to the beach, as a motif from the region of Tuscany shows (figure 148). The painting captures a morning scene with a yellow-tinted sky and a violet sea. Casuarinas are at home in subtropical climates—whether in Australia, Indonesia, Thailand, or the Seychelles. Figure 150 shows a beach on Mauritius.

Under water and on ice

Portholes and other technology-inspired frames suggest views from a submarine and are useful for representations of underwater seascapes. Another possibility is to do away with the architectural frame altogether and to paint the entire wall as if it were a glass pane allowing a view into a huge aquarium. Underwater scenes are always tinted blue, which makes them seem mysterious. Above the surface the view drifts into the distance, but below one gets lost in the nondescript space of the blue. Even the objects that appear close are seen in a blue light—there are no harsh shadows, and sparkling reflections dance unpredictably across all surfaces depending on the speed with which the water moves along the surface. All things are defined in a softer way than above the water in the glare of the unrelenting sun. Toward the background contours quickly grow undefined: a dream world filled with intangible objects. The rich variety of colors and the bizarre forms appear almost surreal; they draw the view into their magical spell.

Figures 152–154 (page 91) show how a coral reef is painted: the strong base colors give depth and a touch of mystery to the painting. When contours are precisely filled in, single shapes

144
Cube-shaped
pavilion, Florida.

145
Lookout point.

146
Access to the
ocean, Florida.

acquire volume. This process is done in several steps and with varying intensities (figure 151, page 90). Dolphins are among the most popular animals. Like the coral reef, a school of dolphins (figure 155, page 92) is developed from the underpainting. Only the three closest dolphins are painted in detail; the others are left increasingly undefined. The animals' spots correspond to the light reflections so that it becomes difficult to distinguish between them. In the upper part of the painting we see the play of the waves on the water surface, seen from below. The underpainting in the lower part of the picture is lighter and more turquoise. This brightness comes from the reflection of the light off the sandy bottom of the sea. The underwater creatures fascinate through their defiance of gravity, and in figure 156, page 92, the jumping dolphins demonstrate the same skill above the surface.

The permanent ice of the arctic (figure 157, page 93) stands in stark contrast to the summer beaches of our dream vacations, but it fascinates

147
Surfer—at home almost anywhere in the world.

148
Pine trees on the Tuscan coast (Golf of Baratti).

149
Fishing boats, Sri Lanka.

150
Casuarinas on Mauritius.

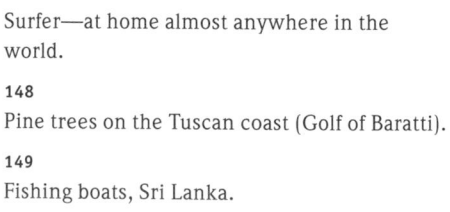

with meditative calm and relaxation in a picture of glacier turquoise, white, and blue. Any motif, be it icy or bucolic, can open our eyes to the matchless beauty of our world.

151
Underwater scene, Great Barrier
Reef, Australia.

152
Underpainting for figure 151.

153, 154
Details are worked out step by
step.

155
School of dolphins in the water.

156
Jumping dolphins.

157
Arctic icebergs.

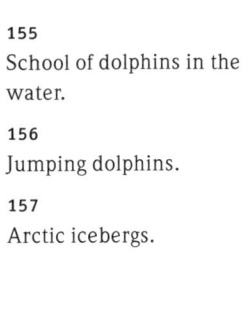

The Authors

Ursula Benad

Martin Benad

Ursula Evelin Benad

studied textile and wall design, a dual interest inspired by a teacher's enthusiasm for Italian fresco paintings. Ursula Benad worked in the textile and fashion industry and as executive for the company Esprit she traveled all over the world, especially to the Far East and the United States. Several years later she opened her own fashion design studio in Düsseldorf and created collections for international companies like Elegance, MCM, and others. Her career was successful and satisfying, but she wished that she could somehow incorporate her painting skills into her work. During a three-month-long stay in Venice she encountered antique painting techniques, frescoes, and illusionistic paintings, even in newly opened stores and restaurants, and decided that she would revive her "old" painting skills, perfect them, and turn them into a new career.

Martin Benad

"My path to color began with philosophy: I was looking for a bridge between feeling and thinking, between experience and understanding," Martin Benad remembers. He studied Waldorf school pedagogy, focusing on Goethe, Steiner, and alternative scientific theories. His musical training as an organist and choirmaster and a study of recitation led to a long career as a creative artist–teacher of liberal arts. He worked on stage and also held seminars on perception training, the psychology of colors, and holistic thinking, which led to many requests for him to design public and private spaces. When he met his future wife in 1993, a road to creative collaboration was opened.

Atelier Benad

focuses on all aspects of color design in architecture, particularly on trompe l'oeil painting, old master techniques, and color psychology. Atelier Benad works with private and corporate clients, including hotels, restaurants, business leaders and other prominent customers. Ursula and Martin Benad interpret traditional forms in a new way, give a personal twist to current trends, and invent an original set of colors and images for each project. As authors of seven books they are outstanding representatives of the field of color design and illusionistic painting. They offer regular seminars in their atelier in Munich, in Tuscany, on the island of Sylt, as well as in other attractive locations. Interior designers, interior architects, artists, painters, and interested laypeople attend to learn new design techniques or to refine their skills. Current seminar and class schedules and an extensive gallery of images are available at: http://www.atelier-benad.de. E-mail: info@atelier-benad.de.

A student in the Atelier-Benad Continuing Education class "Pompeian Decoration."

Master class during the "Sea and Sky" seminar on the island of Sylt.

A group of students in an open-air landscape session in Tuscany.

Scene in studio during the seminar "Illusionistic Painting in Tuscany."